Tom and Bella Stories
Red Series 1

Author   Marlene Greenwood

Illustrator   James Greenwood

© Marlene Greenwood   Author
© James Greenwood   Illustrator

The moral rights of the author and illustrator have been asserted.

This book was originally published as four separate eight-paged books
Titles: *The Big Red Bus*   978 1 84305 227 2
          Cups and Mugs   978 1 84305 228 9
          The Cat-Flap   978 1 84305 233 3
          The Jam Bun   978 1 84305 234 0

All rights reserved. No part of this publication may be reproduced in any form or by any means ... graphic, electronic, or mechanical (including printing, photocopying, recording, taping) or digitally by information storage and retrieval systems ... without prior permission in writing from the copyright holders.

Jelly and Bean Ltd   www.jellyandbean.co.uk

ISBN 978 1 84305 415 3

Tom and Bella Stories Red Series 1

Stories

1 ## The Big Red Bus.......................... page 1

Tom's big red bus goes fast.

2 ## Cups and Mugs............................ page 11

Bella plays with ‹cups and mugs.

3 ## The Cat-Flap................................ page 21

Tigga and Fluff are in trouble.

4 ## The Jam Bun................................ page 31

Tom spills red jam on his top.

Information for Teachers

This book has four separate stories for children learning to read complete sentences.

The vocabulary consists of simple words that are well known to children.

The new letters introduced are **w, ck, j, k, y.**

Words with consonants to blend at their beginning or end are included in the vocabulary.

The text is made up of complete sentences. Capital letters and punctuation are used.

The common words **is, has** are used.

The 'tricky' words used are **the, I, to.**

Story title	New graphemes	High-frequency words to learn
The Big Red Bus	—	big in on is has the
Cups and Mugs	w	on and the up has is
The Cat-Flap	ck	I am is on to get off the but
The Jam Bum	j, y, k	has the on his is in it

Story 1

The Big Red Bus

Tom has a big red bus.

The big red bus has a button.

The big red bus is fast.

The big red bus hits the bin.

The mess hits the cat.

The bus is in the mess.

The cat is on the big red bus.

Tom is mad.

Match the words to the pictures.

Tom is mad.

The bus is fast.

The bus and the mess.

Story 2

Cups and Mugs

Bella has cups and mugs on the mat.

Bella fills the cups on the mat.

Bella fills the mugs on the mat.

The cups drip on the mat.

The mugs drip on the mat.

The pot tips up on the mat.

Bella has a mess on the mat.

Bella is wet.

Can you see a mug?	Can you see a cup?

Can you see the pot?	Can you see Bella?

Story 3

The Cat-Flap

I am Tigga. I am a cat.

I am Fluff. I am a cat.

Tigga is on Tom's bed.

Fluff is on Bella's bed.

Tom tells Tigga to get off the bed.

Bella tells Fluff to get off the bed.

Tigga and Fluff run to the cat-flap.

But Tigga and Fluff get stuck.

Where is Tigga?

Where is Fluff?

Where do Tigga and Fluff get stuck?

Story 4

The Jam Bun

Tom has a red jam bun.

Tom licks the jam.

Yum, yum.

The jam drips on Tom's top.

Tom rubs the jam. His top is a mess.

Tom puts his top in the sink.

Tom rubs it. The top is pink.

Tom puts the top in the sun.

Tom has a red lollipop.

Match the words to the pictures.

Tom licks the bun.

The top is pink.

Tom rubs the jam.

Ingram Content Group UK Ltd.
Milton Keynes UK
UKHW050853020723
424393UK00002B/14